D0057163

Other Books by Thom S. Rainer

Becoming a Welcoming Church
We Want You Here
Who Moved My Pulpit?
I Will
I Am a Church Member
The Millennials (coauthor)
Transformational Church (coauthor)
Simple Life (coauthor)
Essential Church (coauthor)
Vibrant Church (coauthor)
Raising Dad (coauthor)
Simple Church (coauthor)
The Unexpected Journey
Breakout Churches
The Unchurched Next Door
Surprising Insights from the Unchurched
Eating the Elephant (revised edition) (coauthor)
High Expectations
The Every Church Guide to Growth (coauthor)
The Bridger Generation
Effective Evangelistic Churches
The Church Growth Encyclopedia (coeditor)
Experiencing Personal Revival (coauthor)
Giant Awakenings
Biblical Standards for Evangelists (coauthor)
Eating the Elephant
The Book of Church Growth
Evangelism in the Twenty-First Century (editor)

Autopsy
of a
Deceased
Church

12 WAYS TO KEEP YOURS ALIVE

Thom S. Rainer

B&H
PUBLISHING GROUP
Nashville, Tennessee

Copyright © 2014 by Thom S. Rainer
All Rights Reserved
Printed in the United States of America

978-1-4336-8392-3

Published by B&H Publishing Group
Nashville, Tennessee

Dewey Decimal Classification: 262
Subject Heading: CHURCH \ CHURCH RENEWAL \
LEADERSHIP

All Scripture quotations are taken from the Holman Christian
Standard Bible (HCSB) Copyright © 1999, 2000, 2002, 2003,
2009 by Holman Bible Publishers. Used by permission.

11 12 13 14 15 • 23 22 21 20 19

To

My Grandchildren

Canon Rainer
Maggie Rainer
Nathaniel Rainer
Will Rainer
Harper Rainer
Bren Rainer
Joshua Rainer

With many more surely to follow

And always to

Nellie Jo

"Jo Jo" to our grandchildren

Contents

Part 2: Is There Hope for the Dying Church?
Twelve Responses

Acknowledgments

I never expected to write a book about death, whether the subject would be the death of humans or the death of churches. I am hopeful and optimistic by nature. Death and dying, frankly, are subjects I would rather avoid.

But then I wrote a post called "Autopsy of a Deceased Church" on my blog at www.ThomRainer.com. I was amazed at the response. It became and still is my most viewed post. Even months later, people still read that article daily. I knew I had struck a chord.

I first express appreciation to the community of readers at my blog. I know some of you by name, but with millions of viewers a year, I can't know all of you. Thank you, every one of you, for taking time to read what I write. I am still amazed that anyone wants to read my works.

I owe a great deal of appreciation to the B&H team, one of the most capable and excellent teams in publishing today. I wish I could name each of you individually. Thank you Jennifer Lyell and Devin Maddox. You are superb editors, dynamic leaders, and persistent encouragers. And thanks to the two top leaders of B&H: Selma Wilson and Cossy Pachares. You have taken a sleeping giant and turned it into a mighty force in Christian publishing.

There are no words adequate to thank "Team Rainer" in the president's office. I love having "A" players on my team. I am blessed to have three "A+" players: Amy Jordan, Amy Thompson, and Jonathan Howe. They are the brains and hearts behind my social media, my organizational life, and all that I write. Thank you, team.

If you know me at all, you know I love my family. I love my wife, Nellie Jo. I love my sons, Sam, Art, and Jess. I love my daughters-in-law, Erin, Sarah, and Rachel. And I love my seven grandchildren whose names are at the forefront on the dedication page. I fully expect more grandchildren will be on the way by the time this book is published. No pressure.

Though I stand amazed that any of you readers would actually read my publications, I thank you for it. And though I don't know what expectations, hopes, or burdens you bring to the reading of this book, I pray God will use it greatly for you and your congregations.

Ultimately, my greatest gratitude goes to my Lord. This book is about His church. He cares about His church. He loves His church. I pray that my simple words will be used in some small way to help His churches in His power and strength. And if this tome is used in such a way, I know where the credit will go and to Whom the glory belongs.

PART 1

The Autopsy

CHAPTER 1

Introduction

I knew the patient before she died.

It was ten years ago. She was very sick at the time, but she did not want to admit it.

There was only a glimmer of hope at best. But that hope could become a reality only with radical change. She wasn't nearly ready for that change. Indeed, she was highly resistant to any change. Even though she was very sick.

Even though she was dying.

I told her the bad news bluntly: You are dying. I hope I said those words with some compassion. I did feel badly sharing the news. But it was the only way I could see to get her attention.

I even told her that, at best, she had five years to live. At the time I said those words, I don't really think I was that optimistic. I would not have been surprised if she died within the year.

But she was not only in denial; she was in angry denial.

"I'll show you," she said. "I'll prove you are wrong. I am not dying."

Her words were fierce. Defiant. Angry.

It was time for me to leave. I had done all I could.

I left.

I was not angry. I was sad. Very sad.

Now to her credit, she was right up to a point. She did not die in five years. She proved resilient and survived another ten years. But her last decade, though she was technically alive, was filled with pain, sickness, and despair.

I'm not so sure her longer-term survival was a good thing.

She never got better. She slowly and painfully deteriorated.

And then she died.

The Autopsy

She, of course, is a church. A real church. A church in the Midwest.

A church that was probably born out of vision.

A church that died because she no longer had a vision.

I was the church's consultant over a decade ago. The church had reached its peak attendance many years earlier. The worship attendance of 750 in 1975 took place during "the good old days." We'll talk about those days shortly.

By the time I arrived, the attendance had fallen to an average of eighty-three. The large sanctuary seemed to swallow the small crowd on Sunday morning.

The reality was that most of the members did not want me there. They were not about to pay a consultant to tell them what they refused to hear. Only when a benevolent member offered to foot my entire bill did the congregation grudgingly agree to retain me.

I worked with the church for three weeks. The problems were obvious. The solutions were difficult.

On my last day the benefactor walked me to my rental car. "What do you think, Thom?" he asked. He could see the uncertainty in my expression, so he clarified. "How long can our church survive?" That was the moment I gave my foreboding declaration of five years at most.

Of course, I was wrong on the exact number of years. The church has only recently closed. Like many dying churches, it held on to life tenaciously. The church lasted ten years after my declaration of a terminal diagnosis.

My friend from that church called me a week after the church officially closed its doors. We talked for over an hour. I took no pleasure in discovering that my diagnosis was correct. Together, my friend and I reviewed the past ten or more years. We were able to piece together a fairly accurate autopsy.

We learned with even more clarity why the church died. We performed an autopsy.

It was not fun, but we thought it was necessary.

Why Go Through the Pain?

My sister died before I was born. I only recently learned that my father convinced the attending doctor to perform an autopsy, and that he convinced the doctor to let him be in the room while the autopsy was performed. My grieving father had to know why his beloved Amy died. He had to know why her little heart had failed.

He had to know. He just had to know.

Why should I take you through the pain of discovering why churches die?

Because we need to know.

Autopsies are performed on humans to find out why they died. The discoveries might give surviving family members information they need to avoid the same path as their loved one.

Sometimes a forensic pathologist performs an autopsy to discover how a murder was committed, or how an accident happened. The information is always useful. It sometimes brings people to justice.

But that does not mean autopsies are pleasant.

I plan to take you through the results of fourteen church autopsies. I won't bore you with a church-by-church report because there is much redundancy. I will instead summarize my findings of all the deceased churches.

I owe much gratitude to those who talked with me freely and openly, those who performed the autopsies with me. Each of them was a member of a church that was once alive, but now is dead. Each of them went through the pain of an autopsy with me.

The churches are diverse in their denominational or non-denominational backgrounds. They are diverse in their locations. They are diverse in their local and regional demographics.

But they are all similar in one significant way: they followed paths that caused them to die.

Jesus told Peter that the Church will never die: "And I also say to you that you are Peter, and on this rock I will build My church, and the forces of Hades will not overpower it" (Matt. 16:18). Indeed the Church will never die. But churches have and are dying.

It is my prayer that these autopsies, though painful to watch, will prove helpful to leaders and laity of churches today. As many as 100,000[1] churches in America are showing signs of decline toward death.

May God give us the courage to make the changes necessary to give new life to our churches.

The Prayerful Commitment

In every chapter, you will be asked a simple question: "Will you make a prayerful commitment?"

The commitment is really between you and God. Perhaps God will raise up an army of church members who are no longer satisfied with business as usual.

The trauma of observing an autopsy is only beneficial if it is received as a warning to the living. This book is not about dwelling on the past, but bearing fruit in the future. The prayer commitment in each chapter is a positive challenge to take the hill, so to speak, where others may have failed. The commitments are vital in this book. Because if we heed the warnings of the autopsy, we stand to benefit far greater than we could otherwise imagine.

Prayerful Commitment 1

God, open my eyes that I might see my church as You see it. Let me see where change needs to take place, even if it is painful to me. And use me, I pray, to be an instrument of that change whatever the cost.

Questions for Further Thought

1. If your church was given a "physical exam" today, what do you think the doctor's diagnosis would be: healthy, slightly sick, very sick, or dying? Why? *Very sick / slightly sick*

2. Why do many church members in dying churches refuse to see the decline in the health of the church? *They want to be buried there*

3. Explain how churches can die in the context of Matthew 16:18, which says Hades will not prevail. *Hades will not prevail even tho churches die Jesus o...*

Note

1. This number is based on the foundational research for my book *Breakout Churches.*

CHAPTER 2

Slow Erosion

I had not been home in years. My mom died in 1997, and she was the last surviving member of our family to live in our hometown. Because I had no immediate family there, I really had no reason to return.

But I did return more than a decade later. I was stunned. The level of deterioration surpassed my worst imagination.

From my perspective, my small hometown was looking more like a ghost town. Several businesses on the main street were closed and vacant. You could see the faint outline of paint on the glass that once told the name of the store. I walked store by store. My childhood memories came alive.

Now to be sure, the town was never a bustle of activity. Back in the 1960s and 1970s, most people called the town "quaint." It was kind of Mayberry-like, for all you Andy

Griffith fans. It seemed to be a good place to grow up, though the amenities were few.

I looked in the display windows of the closed stores. Dust and more dust were all I could see on the floor and the bare display shelves. Each store brought back a vivid memory. Each step took me back to another time, a better time for this town.

But the overall state of the town was sad, very sad. I knew the place was not what it was in my childhood years, but it was much worse than I expected. I decided to go to one of two fast-food places of my childhood. It too was closed. It looked like it had not been occupied in a decade.

Later that day, I spoke with an acquaintance who had lived there all his life. He was in his mid-sixties. I tend to be straight-forward in my conversations, so I bluntly asked him what happened to our hometown. His perplexed look and simple question said it all: "What do you mean?"

He did not notice the deterioration. He did not see the ghost town that I saw. His perspective was day-by-day. You don't see much change in a day. You don't see the accumulation of dust in hours. For him, it was still largely the same town of a half-century earlier. For him, not much had changed.

The Slow Erosion of Churches

It is rare for a long-term church member to see erosion in his or her church. Growth may come rapidly, but decline is usually slow, imperceptibly slow. This slow erosion is the worst type of decline for churches, because the members have no sense of urgency to change. They see the church on a regular basis; they don't see the gradual decline that is taking place before their eyes.

Often the decline is in the physical facilities, but it is much more than that. The decline is in the vibrant ministries that once existed. The decline is in the prayer lives of the members who remain. The decline is in the outward focus of the church. The decline is in the connection with the community. The decline is in the hopes and dreams of those who remain.

Decline is everywhere in the church, but many don't see it.

Decline Back in Time

Go back in time with me to 520 BC. I know, that's a long time ago. But the story is still relevant. It's told in the Old Testament book of Haggai.

A ragtag remnant of Jews had returned to Jerusalem after a long exile. They returned to a devastated town, but they began to rebuild. Their first order of business was to build the temple, the house of God. They began by laying the foundation. But they stopped working on the temple and began working on their own homes for their own comfort. For a decade they did no work on the house of God.

Imagine the temple. Imagine the house of God. See the dirt accumulating on the foundation. See the vines and overgrowth beginning to cover it. See the decline.

Then God speaks.

He wants to know why the Jews did not notice the decline. God wants to know why they stopped building the temple.

> "The LORD of Hosts says this: These people say: The time has not come for the house of the LORD to be rebuilt. . . . Is it a time for you yourselves to live in your paneled houses, while this house lies in ruins?" (Hag. 1:2–4)

God was angry. His house must be built. It cannot lie in ruins.

> "'. . . When you brought the harvest to your house, I ruined it. Why?' This is the declaration of the LORD of Hosts: 'Because My house still lies in ruins, while each of you is busy with his own house.'" (Hag. 1:9)

Wow.

Over 2,500 years ago, the people of God had neglected building the house of God. It seems as if slow erosion was a problem with them too.

God didn't like it then.

He still doesn't.

Prayerful Commitment 2

God, please let me be part of the solution and not the problem. Show me what I need to see. Open my eyes to Your reality. And give me the courage to move forward in the directions You desire.

Questions for Further Thought

1. What was your church like twenty years ago versus today? Talk with others to get an honest assessment. Do you see any signs of gradual erosion? *Yes, Pastor Matthews I had talked about the Bell Curve. we are*

2. How is the neglect of building the temple described in Haggai 1 like gradual erosion today? *trying but people interest*

3. What do you think God meant in Haggai 1:9 by the phrase "while each of you is busy with his own house"?

His own house. flood Covid & retirement Pastoral

CHAPTER 3

The Past Is the Hero

Before we begin to see the results of the autopsy, please keep this perspective in mind. There were several points where these churches could have reversed the decline they were experiencing. But the remaining members in the church refused to see reality. They were blinded to the slow erosion that was taking place.

Most of the churches in America that close don't shut the doors over a single or few cataclysmic events. In most of the cases, indeed all of them I studied, the issue was slow erosion. There would be no autopsy to perform if they had faced reality and, in God's power, reversed course.

But they didn't.

And for that reason, we must look at them after their death.

The Autopsy: The Common Thread

The most pervasive and common thread of our autopsies was that the deceased churches lived for a long time with the past as hero. They held on more tightly with each progressive year. They often clung to things of the past with desperation and fear. And when any internal or external force tried to change the past, they responded with anger and resolution: "We will die before we change."

And they did.

Hear me clearly: these churches were not hanging on to biblical truths. They were not clinging to clear Christian morality. They were not fighting for primary doctrines, or secondary doctrines, or even tertiary doctrines. As a matter of fact, they were not fighting for doctrines at all.

They were fighting for the past. The good old days. The way it used to be. The way we want it today.

For sure, there were some prophets and dissenters in these churches. They warned others that, if the church did not change, it would die. But the stalwarts did not listen. They fiercely resisted. The dissenters left. And death came closer and closer.

Everyone Loves a Hero

"Hero" is usually a good word. It speaks of a man or woman who has done something remarkable, something courageous, something worth noting.

Men and women who fight for our country are heroes. They risk their lives for our freedom and safety.

First responders, like police, firefighters, and other emergency personnel are heroes. They keep our communities safe. They protect us. They do so often at the risk of their wellbeing or even their lives.

I love reading Hebrews 11. Most Bible editors have inserted the subtitle "Heroes of Faith" for this chapter. There is Abel who offered God a better sacrifice. Enoch who was taken away before death. Noah who built an ark. Abraham who went where God said even though he did not know where that was. Sarah who conceived at an impossible old age. Isaac who blessed a future generation. Joseph who remembered the exodus of the Israelites. Moses who left Egypt for a promised land.

And Rahab. Gideon. Barak. Samson. Jephthah. David. Samuel. The prophets.

According to the writer of Hebrews, all of these men and women were heroes of faith because they obeyed God even though they did not know the consequences of that obedience. They saw themselves as foreigners of this land and life, temporary residents of the earth (v. 13).

They sacrificed their comfort, their homes, their ways of life, and their possessions because they knew that this life was only temporary, that a better and eternal life awaited them.

The "good old days" did not exist in their minds. The future held the best days. They understood that this life is not a time to get comfortable.

When the Past Is Hero

I got an e-mail today from someone who was really mad. I guess he was mad at me, but I'm not sure why. He described American churches as they were in the 1970s and 1980s, perhaps earlier. He was mad about music styles. He was mad about church architecture. He was mad about audio speakers and big screens. He was mad about "appropriate" church attire.

Yep, he was really mad. He should have written someone other than me. Ask my sons. I'm neither cool nor contemporary.

For him, the past was his hero. He was clinging, hanging on to things of this world. And because it was slipping away, he was angry, hurt, and probably fearful.

Don't get me wrong. There is much to revere and remember about the past. I am grateful for those who came before me. I am grateful for events and people of the past that shaped my life.

I remember my parents whose influence will never wane despite their deaths.

I remember a high school football coach who shared the gospel with me.

I remember a friend who went to Vietnam, but did not return. He died for our nation, including me.

I remember the church where I was baptized in Anniston, Alabama. It seems that everything that took place in that church is a part of my "good old days."

Yes, we respect the past. At times we revere the past. But we can't live in the past.

Signs of Past Heroes

Do you know the name Harry Truman? Let me be clearer. Do you know the name Harry Randall Truman? No, he was not a former president. He was a homeowner at the foot of Mount St. Helens in Washington state. In 1980, the volcanic mountain was showing signs of a major eruption. Indeed one expert declared that the chance of a major eruption was virtually 100 percent.

Truman's home was located at the south end of Spirit Lake at the foot of the mountain. He was living in the most likely path of the volcanic flow. He was facing an almost certain death.

Governmental officials implored him to leave. Friends told him that his failure to move was tantamount to suicide. Family members begged him to leave lest he die.

On May 18, 1980, the massive eruption took place. The lava flowed right in the projected path of Truman's home.

On May 18, 1980, Harry Randall Truman died.

He just could not let go of his home, even if it meant certain death.

So what did the deceased churches cling to? What did they refuse to let go of facing certain death?

Worship styles were certainly on the list. As were fixed orders of worship services. And times of worship services.

Some stubbornly held on to buildings and rooms, particularly if that room or building was a memorial, named for one of the members of the past.

Some would not accept any new pastor except that one pastor who served thirty years ago.

But more than any one item, these dying churches focused on their own needs instead of others. They looked inwardly instead of outwardly. Their highest priorities were the way they've always done it, and that which made them the most comfortable.

It was not just the past they revered. It was their personal good old days.

So, unlike the heroes of Hebrews 11 who held onto nothing of this life, these dying churches held onto everything, at least everything that made them comfortable and happy.

Such is the reason we speak of them in the past.

They were warned. They were facing certain death. They saw every sign.

But like Harry Randall Truman, they preferred death to change.

And death is what they got.

Prayerful Commitment 3

God, give me the conviction and the courage to be like the heroes of Hebrews 11. Teach me not to hold onto those things in my church that are my personal preferences and styles. Show me not only how to let go, but where to let go, so that I may heed Your commands more closely.

Questions for Further Thought

1. Are there any areas in your church where you are resisting change simply because of your own preferences?

Not really. I came 12 years ago.

2. What is the common theme among the heroes of Hebrews 11?

3. Look at Hebrews 11:13–16 and discuss it in light of churches that die holding onto the past.

CHAPTER 4

The Church Refused to Look Like the Community

Our autopsy revealed this condition in several of the fourteen churches. Look at the faces of the members before the church officially died. Now look at the faces of most of the people who live in the community where the church is located. They are significantly different.

Here is the typical scenario I heard. In the "good old days" the church was booming as residents in the community flocked to the church. The church was a part of the community and it reflected the community.

Then the community began to change. In some cases the change was ethnic or racial. In other cases it was age-related. And sometimes it was simply socioeconomic change.

But the change was real and the members of the church felt it.

The response to the changing community was often subtle. One family in the church would decide to "move up" to another section of town. Others would follow. The migration of people in and out of the church was often slow and almost impercep-tible. But it was very real.

For two to three decades the church held its own. While it was not reaching the new residents of the community, the members were not leaving in mass either. They were willing to drive into the community where they once lived because, after all, it was their church.

But their children, and especially their grandchildren, did not respond accordingly. Some of these younger generations left town completely. Others stayed in the areas, but they found churches where their homes were. They did not see the point in driving to a transitioned community that had no identity with the church.

So the church began its death march. Family by family the church declined. Of course, the membership of the church grew older. Those who once lived in the community represented the oldest of the members, and no younger families replaced them.

For sure, there would be an occasional but faint attempt to reach the community. Essentially, on those rare occasions they tried to reach out, the church members asked the community residents to come to them, to the church. There was almost never any effort to go into the community.

And no one, at any point, ever mentioned the possibility of a willingness to turn over the leadership of the church to the residents of the community. What may seem like common sense to an outsider was treasonous to the church members.

After all, it was their church. The community members had never given a dime to the congregation. Why would they ever consider letting those outsiders take over the church?

The Church Becomes a Fortress

What imagery comes to your mind when you hear the word "fortress"? A medieval castle? Fort Knox? Huge buildings with gates and locks and moats? Something that is almost impossible for the outside world to enter?

Any of those word pictures will work. The key is to keep people and possessions on the inside safe, and to keep people on the other side out.

If you talk to members in a dying church, most will deny that their church is a fortress. But in our autopsy, we found that is exactly what was taking place. People in the community did not feel welcome in the church. Those in the church were more concerned about protecting the way they did church than reaching residents of the community.

You see, these churches really were fortresses. The very thought of making significant changes to reach and impact the community is frightening. To suggest that the church members begin to transition leadership to residents of the community seems absurd. It is our fortress, they say. Outsiders not welcome. We will fight to keep the church just as it is until we die.

And that day is not very far away.

Others First = Life. Me First = Death.

When a church ceases to have a heart and ministry for its community, it is on the path toward death. Whenever local churches are mentioned in the New Testament, they are always exhorted to be other-centered.

Paul told the church at Philippi to look after the interests of others even as it considered its own interests: "If then there is any encouragement in Christ, if any consolation of love, if any fellowship with the Spirit, if any affection and mercy, fulfill my joy by thinking the same way, having the same love, sharing the same feelings, focusing on one goal. Do nothing out of rivalry or conceit, but in humility consider others as more important than yourselves. Everyone should look out not only for his own interests, but also for the interests of others" (Phil. 2:1–4).

Did you get that? Vibrant and living churches look after the interests of others. They are concerned for their communities. They open the door for others.

But dying churches are concerned with self-preservation. They are concerned with a certain way of doing church. They are all about self. Their doors are closed to the community. And even more sadly, most of the members in the dying church would not admit they are closed to those God has called them to reach and minister.

Our autopsy revealed, that at some point in its history, the church stopped reaching and caring for the community.

How could we tell? The church did not look like or reflect the community in which it was located. Or if it did, it stopped ministering to those around them.

God called the church to look outwardly.

Our autopsy revealed that the church had become self-centered and self-gratifying.

Prayerful Commitment 4

God, give my church and me a heart for our community. Let me see the people through Your eyes. And give me the courage and the wisdom to let go of this church, so that others who best reflect this community can lead us and teach us.

Questions for Further Thought

1. Does your church try to reach and minister to its community, even to the point of giving up authority to better reach the people? Explain your "yes" or "no."

2. When does a church act like a fortress?

3. How does Paul's exhortation to the Philippian church relate to churches today impacting their communities?

CHAPTER 5

The Budget Moved Inwardly

When you conduct the autopsy of a church, you must follow the money. For where the money of the church goes, so goes its heart.

Indeed you can see in the budgets of the deceased churches over several years that predictable patterns begin to emerge. And, as you probably can imagine, members in the dying churches have no idea that a financial death march is slowly taking place.

When Wellington R. Burt died in 1919, he was known as one of the wealthiest people in America. He had amassed a fortune as a lumber baron. Indeed, he was listed at number eight among America's richest persons. He also had political power. He had served as mayor of Saginaw, Michigan, and as a state senator for Michigan.

And he was greedy. Very greedy.

His will was a near perfect reflection of his greed. He stated that no one could receive a dollar of his estate until twenty-one years after the death of the last surviving grandchild. In other words, he didn't want the family he knew to get any of his money. Many tried, but the courts held the legitimacy of his greedy will and life.

In 2011, distributions were finally made to a dozen relatives Burt never knew, ninety-two years after his death.

Burt's physical remains are in a fifteen-foot-high mausoleum in Saginaw. It is fortified as if he tried to have an iron grip on his death, much like the tight-fisted ways of his life.

Churches Too

I never met a member of a dying church who thought his or her church was greedy. I certainly never met one who thought their greed compared to such miserable recluses as Wellington Burt.

And I'm not even sure if greed is the best descriptor of these churches. Perhaps it is better to say that their funds are inwardly focused.

For example, in many of the deceased churches, the personnel portion of the budget steadily increased over the years. It was not that the churches were paying their staff more; rather the personnel portion of the budget increased proportionally to the declining total each year.

The churches had less to spend, but personnel costs were often the last to be cut.

Why?

Because the church members viewed the staff as their personal caretakers. Those who were paid by the church were supposed to spend most, if not all, of their time visiting the members, counseling the members, attending functions with the members, and so on.

Don't get me wrong, in vibrant churches the staff often meets the needs of the members. That is part of their God-given calling. But in the dying churches, the staff is expected to almost exclusively be on call for church members.

That means staff members aren't reaching out to others beyond the church. That means they aren't involved in the community in an incarnational sense. That means they are mostly hired hands for church members.

It is for that reason the budget for personnel is often the last to go.

Likewise, building and facility costs are reduced only as a last resort. We'll look at that issue more fully in chapter 11. Just keep in mind this truism: In dying churches the last expenditures to be reduced are those that keep the members most comfortable.

Where Are the Cuts Made?

It is fascinating to look at twenty consecutive annual budgets of churches that closed. In the few churches where we were able to get budgets, we had a clearer understanding of why the churches eventually died.

Follow the money.

Look at the line items in the budget. See where the cuts were made.

Our autopsy revealed, in most cases, cuts were made to ministries and programs with outward foci. So a particular ministry to the community is no longer essential. Funds to reach beyond the church are no longer available. The decision is justified by declining receipts. Fair enough. But notice that the outreach and community ministries are the first to go.

Not those ministries for church members. Not at first anyway.

The Rich Young Ruler and Deceased Churches

You've read the text many times. You've heard it preached and taught.

A wealthy man approaches Jesus and asks Him what he must do to inherit eternal life. Jesus starts with some of the Ten Commandments. Then, in Mark 10:21–22, this exchange takes place: "Then, looking at him, Jesus loved him and said to him,

'You lack one thing: Go, sell all you have and give to the poor, and you will have treasure in heaven. Then come, follow Me.' But he was stunned at this demand, and he went away grieving, because he had many possessions."

Did you get that?

The man could not let go. He was not merely sad at the prospect of letting go. The text said he *grieved* at the thought of giving up his possessions.

We hold on to things because we want our way of life. Our comfort. Our possessions.

That's what happens to churches that die. They spend for their way of doing church. Their comfort. Their possessions.

Follow the money. You will learn much about a church.

By the way, not all the deceased churches died broke. In fact, a few of them had quite a treasure chest when they died. Some had inherited funds. Others had accumulated funds.

You don't have to be broke to be dying. It's not a matter of how much you have. It's what you do with your money, or what your attitude is about the money. Some churches hold on to funds because the money itself becomes the focus. They no longer ask how the church can make a difference for the Kingdom with the money. They accumulate because they fear not having enough money.

Like the rich young ruler, they grieve at the thought of doing something with the money for someone beyond themselves. They fear they will not have enough money if they do.

So they die with "enough" money.

The Autopsy Was Clear and Revealing

In all the churches we autopsied, a financial pattern developed over time. The pattern was one where funds were used more to keep the machinery of the church moving, and to keep the members happy, than funding the Great Commission and the Great Commandment.

The money, though, was symptomatic of a heart problem. The church cared more for its own needs than the community and the world.

And no church can sustain such an inward focus indefinitely. It will eventually die of heart failure.

Prayerful Commitment 5

Lord, help me to grasp that all the money I think I have is really Yours. Help me to grasp that all the money our church has is not the church's, but Yours. Give us healthy giving hearts to use these funds according to Your purpose.

Questions for Further Thought

1. How would the budget and use of funds of a healthy church differ from that of a dying church?

2. How does the story of the rich young ruler in Mark 10 inform us about how a church might view the money it has?

3. What are some ways churches can move their use of funds from predominantly an inward focus to an outward focus?

CHAPTER 6

The Great Commission Becomes the Great Omission

When the past is hero, as we noted in chapter 3, certain symptoms develop. These symptoms can become sicknesses themselves, sicknesses that lead to death. Some churches begin with a great heart and a great effort toward the Great Commission.

But the methods used become the focus rather than the Great Commission itself. As a consequence, the Great Commission becomes the Great Omission.

I live in Nashville, Tennessee. It is one incredible place to live. Indeed, it is the best place I have ever lived. There was a time that I had retirement plans elsewhere, but I can't ever see myself leaving. God willing, when I get to retirement age, I'll continue to live in this place that has really become my home.

There is so much to this city, but the musical talent is almost beyond belief. Nashville is the epicenter of both Christian and country music.

One of my favorite country singers is Alan Jackson. He has countless hits, but one of my favorites is "Remember When." The song is written from the perspective of an older man to his wife as he recounts all the times they have experienced together, both good and bad. It is a sweet song that ends with these lyrics: "Remember when we said when we turned gray, when the children grow up and move away. We won't be sad, we'll be glad for all the life we've had. And we'll remember when."

Nostalgia can be good. It can be fun and healthy. We certainly need to "remember when." But, as I noted earlier, we can't live in the past, and we can't re-create the past. We do "remember when," but we move on.

Our autopsy revealed a lot of nostalgia about the growth of the church. There was a lot of "remember when" about particular years of growing numbers and high attendance days. However, members of dead or dying churches often overlook the reason behind those years of growth and expansion. Thriving churches have the Great Commission as the centerpiece of their vision, while dying churches have forgotten the clear command of Christ.

Great Commission Amnesia

There are a number of New Testament passages where Jesus sends out His followers. The text that is used most often to refer to the Great Commission is Matthew 28:19–20: "Go, therefore, and make disciples of all nations, baptizing them in the name of the Father and of the Son and of the Holy Spirit, teaching them to observe everything I have commanded you. And remember, I am with you always, to the end of the age."

The imperative in those verses is "go." But as we go, there are several sub-commands. We are to make disciples. We are to baptize. We are to teach.

Those are a lot of action words.

But the deceased church, somewhere in its history, forgot to act upon the Great Commission. So they stopped going. And making disciples. And baptizing them. And teaching them.

Perhaps I'm being too gentle to say the deceased church "forgot" to act upon the Great Commission. Perhaps it is more accurate to say the church "decided" not to act upon Christ's command.

You see, the Great Commission requires at least two points of obedience from church members. They are to go, and they are to depend totally upon the power of Christ. That's why Jesus reminded them: "I am with you always." Christ was ready and willing to work through them. Indeed Jesus commanded it.

But the deceased church, in its past, stopped going. And it stopped depending on Christ.

Why?

"Going" in Christ's power requires effort. Certainly the results are dependent upon Him, but obedience is work. And obedience in His power means that we are praying to Jesus so we can reach others. That requires an "other" focus. That requires us to look beyond ourselves. That requires us to get uncomfortable. That requires us to go.

As I looked at the deaths of fourteen churches, I saw a common pattern. Obedience to the Great Commission faded; it usually faded gradually. It's not like one day the church was sending out dozens of members in the community and it suddenly stopped. Instead the decline in the outward focus was gradual, almost imperceptibly gradual.

It was like the slow erosion described in chapter 2. The efforts at obedience to the Great Commission faded gradually, so that no one noticed. Or if someone did notice, he or she was largely ignored. The more vocal members usually left the church. The comfortable members remained behind for the deathwatch.

So perhaps "Great Commission amnesia" is really too kind. Perhaps that description implies that the members were not at fault, that they no longer had the ability to recall or know what they were supposed to do.

Perhaps it would be more truthful to say these dying churches had "Great Commission disobedience." They chose not to remember what to do. They chose their own comfort over reaching others with the gospel.

That is why the autopsy results concluded that the Great Commission became the great omission.

The Convenient Omission of the Action Words

Related to the great omission is the nature of conversations among church members of dying churches. These members, as we have noted earlier, often fixate on the good old days. And those days in their memories include some spectacular results:

- A high attendance day that often marked the peak of the church.
- Dozens of new members every year.
- Vibrant ministries in the community.
- Recognition for their growth by the denomination or some similar body.

As the members of the dying church recalled those days, often decades earlier, they longed for similar results today. They often wondered why they could not replicate those good old days. And it was not unusual for them to blame others for their plight.

You see, these members had a convenient omission in their recollections. They wanted the same results as yesteryear, but they weren't willing to expend the efforts. Remember the action words from Matthew 28? Go, make disciples, baptize, and teach.

Members of the dying church weren't willing to go into the community to reach and minister to people. They weren't willing to invite their unchurched friends and relatives. They weren't willing to expend the funds necessary for a vibrant outreach.

They just wanted it to happen. Without prayer. Without sacrifice. Without hard work.

But here's the bigger issue. Even if the church began to grow on its own, the members of the dying church would only accept the growth if the new members were like them and if the church would continue to "do church" the way they wanted it.

That reality, when it is all said and done, is likely at the heart of the issue. Members of the dying churches really didn't want growth unless that growth met their preferences and allowed them to remain comfortable.

But the issue of preferences is its own category in reasons churches die. We will look at that issue in the next chapter of the autopsy.

Prayer Commitment 6

Lord, remind me that I am to be a Great Commission Christian in a Great Commission church. Remind me that, in Your strength, I am to do whatever it takes to reach out into my community with the transforming power of the gospel.

Questions for Further Thought

1. Why do most dying churches have members who are nostalgic about the "good old days"? What are the biblical implications of that mind-set?

2. Look at and describe the different parts of Matthew 28:19–20. Is your church more obedient or disobedient to those biblical commands?

3. What is the relationship between Jesus' promise to always be with us in Matthew 28:20, and a mind-set that focuses on one's own comfort?

CHAPTER 7

The Preference-Driven Church

To say the room was tense would be a massive understatement. It was eight years before the death of the church, but few in that room would have predicted the church's demise. The church had bounced back a bit during the past year. Since most of the members would not allow any contemporary elements in the very staid and traditional service at 11:00 a.m., some younger adults started their own contemporary service at 8:30. Bible study classes fit between the two services.

Of course, the 8:30 service was really not that contemporary by modern standards. An acoustic guitar. Some contemporary songs along with the more traditional hymns. A keyboard instead of the organ. But it was really more blended than anything.

The new service did provide the first growth in the church in two decades. The previous year attendance had dipped from seventy-five to sixty-two. But the new service added thirty people in average attendance, so the church was at a five-year high of ninety-two in worship attendance.

As the younger adults invited friends to the first service, they kept hearing the same refrain: "We like the service, but it would be better for us and our children if the service was later."

The solution seemed simple. Move the traditional service to 8:30 and the contemporary service to 11:00.

Wrong.

The change required a church vote. At least that's what some of the members said. No one could find any confirmation. So it was time for the meeting. It was time for the business session from Hades.

There were about 150 people present. That included members who had not been to church in five years or more. That included people most others did not know. It was obvious what was taking place. Members had recruited others to come to the meeting to vote not to change.

The exchange of words was harsh. Accusations were made. Guitars were declared to be "of the devil." One member declared he would let the church die before that change was made.

He would get his way eight years later.

The vote was not close. Nothing changed.

Well, that's not exactly true. The first service ceased five weeks later. Attendance dropped to forty-three by the end of the year. And less than eight years later, the church closed its doors.

Me, Myself, and I

Every one of the fourteen autopsied churches had some level of this problem before they died. A significant number of the members moved the focus from others to themselves. And when a church moves in that direction, it is headed for decline then death. The decline may be protracted, and the death may be delayed.

But it is inevitable. The church will die.

A church cannot survive long-term where members are focused on their own preferences:

- My music style.
- My desired length and order of worship services.
- My desired color and design of buildings and rooms.
- My activities and programs.
- My need of ministers and staff.
- My, my, my.

The Bible contains seemingly unlimited passages on the Christlike attitude all Christians should always have. One of the best descriptions of this attitude was written by the Apostle Paul in Philippians 2:5–11. Keep in mind that this passage is not only a description of the obedience of Christ; it is an example for us to follow.

We are to be servants. We are to be obedient. We are to put others first. We are to do whatever it takes to seek the best for others and our church.

Paul puts it powerfully and cogently: "Make your own attitude that of Christ Jesus." So what did Jesus do?

- He "did not consider equality with God something to be used for His own advantage."
- "He emptied Himself by assuming the form of a slave."
- "He humbled Himself."
- He became "obedient to the point of death—even to death on a cross."

There were not many indications in the autopsied churches that most members had such a self-sacrificial attitude. Instead the attitude was self-serving, self-giving, and self-entitled. It was about me, myself, and I.

Death was thus inevitable.

The lifeblood of a healthy church is one that is more like the mind of Christ in the members' attitudes. Sadly, the dying churches rarely had members who were so other-centered.

The *Love Dare* Story

In 2008 an inconspicuous little book took the world by storm. *The Love Dare* was a book based on the movie *Fireproof,* about a struggling husband trying to save his dying marriage. His dad gives him a little handwritten book that is a forty-day challenge to become a better husband.

No one predicted that the book based on the movie would become a movement. Millions and millions of copies have sold. More importantly, millions of marriages have been saved and strengthened.

The premise of the book is simple. Every day for forty days a husband or wife is to do something selflessly for his or her spouse. The book is a powerful and biblical reminder that, in the relationship of marriage, each party is to seek to look after the interests of his or her spouse.

It's a book about selflessness. Other-centeredness.

That is how we are to enter into relationship with others in the church. Membership in the church is not country club membership. It's not about paying your dues and getting perks.

It's like Paul described in 1 Corinthians 12:12–31. We are members of the body of Christ. We do not exist to serve ourselves; instead, we exist for the greater good of the body.

Members of dying churches did not get that. For most of the members, their affiliation with the church focused around their desires and needs. And, as the church got closer to death, the intensity of their arguments and demands for their preferences grew.

A church by definition is a body of believers who function for the greater good of the congregation. In essence, when church members increasingly demand their own preferences, the church is steadily not becoming the church. It is therefore neither surprising nor unexpected, at least from an observer's point of view, when the church closes its doors.

The church really died before then because its members refused to be the church.

Prayerful Commitment 7

Lord, open my eyes to the needs of others. Show me how to live more like Your Son, who always put others' interests first. And especially show me that attitude as I serve in my church.

Questions for Further Thought

1. What are some unfortunately common areas where church members insist or demand their own preferences? Why do you think that happens?

2. Read 1 Corinthians 12:12–27 and relate the passage to how we are to have the right attitudes and actions in our church.

3. Read Philippians 2:5–11 and compare the attitude of Christ with the attitude of a selfish and entitled church member.

CHAPTER 8

Pastoral Tenure Decreases

I am honored and humbled to hear from pastors. Though none are perfect, I see pastors as some of the most sacrificial and giving people I know.

It is self-evident that pastors and their leadership are vital to churches. The problem is that many good leaders are leaving churches before they reach their prime leadership years at a church. That certainly was the case in the churches we autopsied.

In ten of the fourteen deceased churches, the pattern of pastoral tenure became common. We will address the other four churches in this chapter as well.

For the majority of the churches, pastors came and went at a pace of every two to three years, especially in the two decades leading to the deaths of the churches. The cycle was predictable.

The church was declining. The church would call a new pastor with the hope that the pastor could lead the church back to health. The pastor comes to the church and leads in a few changes. The members don't like the changes and resist. The pastor becomes discouraged and leaves. In some cases, the pastor was fired.

Repeat cycle.

A Story Waiting to Happen

The stories I hear about churches and pastors are sometimes encouraging and sometimes discouraging. I am fearful that the following correspondence is the indication of a not-so-hopeful situation.

The pastor began his e-mail to me:

> I have been pastor of my church for eighteen months. The attendance has declined from 97 to 76 in that time. Each pastor before me was here less than three years, at least the last ten pastors. The only exception was a pastor in the late 1990s who lasted almost five years.

He continued:

> I guess I was like the rest of them. I thought I would be different. I thought my ministry

would not follow the same pattern as the others. It looks like I'm wrong. The pastor search committee told me they were ready for leadership and change; they were ready to move in another direction. Well, I began suggesting some small changes after I got here, and all heck broke loose! I asked one of the members of the search committee why they were so resistant to change, especially since they seem to say otherwise. He kind of shrugged and said that he didn't mean that kind of change, whatever that meant.

The pastor's e-mail concluded with little hope:

I was naïve to think I could change something the other pastors couldn't. I guess I'll be leaving the church soon too. For me, it's both frustration and financial. The church has shrunk to the point that they can't afford my salary. They've cut my pay once. There is no way they can support a fulltime pastor. I just don't see the church making it much longer.

Indeed the church may keep its doors open several more years, but it too seems to be on the death spiral. All signs point that way, particularly the steady rotation of pastors, and the decreasing pay of the current pastor.

The Life Stages of Pastoral Tenure

For more than two decades I have studied, contemplated, and written about the tenure of a pastor. Why is pastoral tenure relatively brief on the average? Does that tenure contain common and distinct stages? Is there a particular point in the tenure when more pastors leave the church?

The more I study the phenomenon of pastoral tenure, the more I am convinced there are distinct stages with clear characteristics. Certainly I understand that there are numbers of exceptions to my delineations. I am also fully aware that the years I designate for each stage are not precise.

Nevertheless, I have some level of confidence in my findings. And each stage has a relationship to the issue of dying churches.

- **Year 1: Honeymoon.** Both pastor and church have a blank slate and they enter the relationship hoping and believing the best about each other. Perhaps the pastor was weary of a previous pastorate, and perhaps the church was happy to replace their former pastor. For a season, neither can do wrong in the other's eyes. That season does not usually last long.

- **Years 2 and 3: Conflicts and Challenges.** No pastor is perfect. No church is perfect. Each party discovers the imperfections after a few months. Like a newlywed couple, they began to have their differences after a while. The spiritual health of both the pastor and the church will likely determine the severity of the conflicts and challenges.

- **Years 4 and 5: Crossroads, Part 1.** This period is one of the most critical in the relationship. If the conflict was severe, the pastor will likely leave or be forced out. Indeed, these years, four and five, are the most common years when a pastor leaves a church. On the other hand, if the pastor and the church manage their relationship well, they can often look forward to some of the best years ahead.

- **Years 6 to 10: Fruit and Harvest.** My research is not complete, but it's more than anecdotal. A church is likely to experience some of its best years, by almost any metrics, during this period of a pastor's tenure. Indeed, in my interviews with both pastors and members, I have heard this theme repeated. Both parties have worked through the tough times. They now trust each other and love each other more deeply.

- **Years 11 and beyond: Crossroads, Part 2.** During the first crossroads era, the pastor decides to stay or leave. Or the congregations may make the decision. During this relatively rare tenure beyond ten years, the pastor will go down one of two paths. One path is to be reinvigorated as a leader and ready to tackle new challenges and cast new visions. Or the pastor will be resistant to change, and then become complacent. I have seen both extremes, but I am still struggling to understand why pastors go down one path versus the other.

Most pastors in dying churches have shorter tenure. Our autopsies revealed that sad trend in ten of the fourteen churches. Indeed most of them left in the second stage of pastoral tenure, conflicts, and challenges. When these pastors initiated or even suggested change, there was fierce resistance. They really didn't see much hope based upon the patterns and the history of the church, so they left.

And the cycle repeated itself until, finally, the church shut its doors.

The Exceptions

Four of the deceased churches had long-term pastorates near or at the end of their lives. They were clearly an exception to the patterns of the other churches.

Why?

The pastor made the decision to adopt the attitude of the recalcitrant members. There was no attempt to lead toward change. There was no attempt to have an outward focus. There was no attempt to become more like the community in which the church was located.

These pastors took the paths of least resistance. They likely knew the church was headed toward demise, or at least toward severe decline.

In the life stages pattern, they do make it to "Crossroads, Part 2," the stage of eleven years and beyond.

But, for these pastors, decline and death of the church was preferable to conflict. They became caretakers of members only. They sided with the members at any hint of change.

Three of the four pastors reached retirement age when the churches closed the doors. The other pastor was able to get a staff position at another church.

But in all cases, the churches died.

Prayerful Commitment 8

God, please give our pastor a heart and a vision to reach and minister to people beyond our own walls. Teach me to be the kind of church member who encourages and supports our pastor, so discouragement and disillusionment does not lead to departure.

Questions for Further Thought

1. Describe the typical cycle of pastoral tenure in a dying church. Why does this pattern develop? How can it be reversed?

2. Look at the life stages of pastoral tenure and identify which of the two stages are more common in a dying church. Why is pastoral tenure even important in any church?

3. Paul told Timothy to fulfill his ministry by "do[ing] the work of an evangelist" (2 Tim. 4:5). What challenges would a pastor of a dying church have to fulfill this mandate?

CHAPTER 9

The Church Rarely
Prayed Together

T he man sitting across from me was not enjoying the
moment. We were talking about a church he loved. Indeed
the small group of two men and three women seemed ill at ease.

We were talking about a church that died four years earlier.
Mike was the first to respond.

He still referred to it as "his" church. He was still having
trouble letting go. He was still grieving.

The last thing a grieving person needs is to be a part of an
autopsy. But he agreed to do so with the hope that the process
could help some other churches in the future. I told him that
was the hope and purpose of this book.

So he answered my questions. He added insights. He spoke slowly, methodically, like a person who was still grieving.

Because he was.

The Question

I asked him the question I asked all of the survivors of the deceased churches.

Did the church members pray together?

Inevitably they paused. They weren't sure how to answer the question.

You see, most of the churches, almost to the day they shut the doors, had some type of prayer time. It may have been a part of the worship services. It may have been with some type of fellowship like a Wednesday evening meal.

Sure, we prayed together. The answer came in unanimity but not with much enthusiasm. So I probed further.

Describe your prayer times, I requested.

That's where the revelation would come. That's where we discovered together the question behind the question. As they began to describe their prayer times together, they began to understand more clearly. Let's listen in on one of those conversations, one that was representative of most of the responses.

The Response

Dorothy spoke next.

"Oh yes," she said. "We prayed together as a church. We had a Wednesday night meal and prayer time. When we were larger, we were able to afford cooks to prepare our meals. But as we lost members, we had to go to potluck. That was a shame, because you never knew what the other people would bring. I remember one night when we had twelve vegetables and one dessert. No meat. No bread. That was a shame."

She had gotten off topic, so I guided her back. "Tell me about the prayer time on Wednesday night," I asked.

"Well," she began somewhat thoughtfully, "Carl would pass out a prayer list to all of us." I interrupted her since I did not know Carl. She continued, "Carl was a deacon and he had a copy machine at his office. We used to have a church secretary type and copy those, but we had to let her go because we couldn't afford her. Carl just kind of picked up the slack there. You know, it was a sad day when we no longer had a full-time secretary. That was a shame."

Again, I ask her to return to the topic of prayer.

"That's pretty much it," she said. "Carl would pass out the prayer list, and one person would have the blessing and pray for those on the list. Then we would eat. Of course one time we had no meat or bread. That was a shame."

When Eyes Open

It was at that point that I asked the questions: Do you really think that was a meaningful time of prayer? Do you think that's how the New Testament churches prayed?

Inevitably there would be a pause and then an admission. No, they said. It was more like a routine or ritual. It would hardly qualify as corporate prayer in the New Testament sense.

And then they would reflect. Their eyes would open. They would remember those days when church members came together for powerful times of prayer. Some recalled twenty-four-hour prayer emphases the churches had. Those "good old days" of prayer typically coincided with the best days of the churches, at least to the best of their recollection.

Not coincidently, prayer and the health of the church went hand in hand. When the church is engaged in meaningful prayer, it becomes both the cause and the result of greater church health.

A New Testament Example

It was the first church, the Jerusalem church. Many had become Christians and they began to gather together in places at Jerusalem. Luke, with his eye for detail and historical accuracy, describes the early days of this church in Acts 2:42: "And they devoted themselves to the apostles' teaching, to fellowship, to the breaking of bread, and to prayers."

We could spend volumes on this one verse, but note what the early followers of Christ found important: the apostles' teaching (the Word of God), the fellowship and the breaking of bread (each other), and the prayers.

Don't read too quickly past the word "devoted" in Acts 2:42. The word meaning has much intensity and deliberation. It is like a wild and hungry beast ready to devour its prey. When the early Jerusalem church members devoted themselves to prayer, they were doing a lot more than reading names off a list. They were fervent, intense, and passionate about prayer. They had no doubt that God was listening and responding. A failure to pray was tantamount to a failure to breathe.

Prayer was not an add-on to give them permission to eat a meal. It was serious stuff for a serious group of church members.

Prayer was the lifeblood of the early church.

But Not the Deceased Churches

He paused when I asked the same questions. He was no different than the others who had graciously given of their time for these autopsies. But he did not have a ready answer to the questions: Do you really think that was a meaningful time of prayer? Do you think that's how the New Testament churches prayed?

After a short pause, he said something very telling. "There was a day when prayer was powerful in our church," he began. "People would pray before the worship services. Small groups spent a lot of time in prayer. We prayed intensely for our community."

"Then," he stopped. It was like a light when on. "Then our community started changing," he spoke methodically and slowly. "We were afraid. Many members sold their homes and got out as quickly as they could. We started focusing on the fear. We stopped serving the community."

"And . . ." Tears welled in his eyes. He started again. "And we stopped praying with the passion we once had. That's it. That was the beginning of the decline that led to our death. We stopped taking prayer seriously. And the church started dying."

No prayer. No hope. And the church started dying.

Prayerful Commitment 9

Lord, teach me to pray. Teach me to pray consistently. Teach me to be a leader in prayer in my church. And teach me to keep passionate and believing prayer as the lifeblood of this church.

Questions for Prayerful Thought

1. Most churches have times of prayer. What is the difference between those churches that have meaningful prayer and those churches that do not?

2. Why would a church's failure to engage in meaningful prayer lead to its demise?

3. What is the role and place of prayer in the early Jerusalem church in the context of Acts 2:41–47?

CHAPTER 10

The Church Had No
Clear Purpose

I t is considered one of the greatest American victories in
the history of the Olympics. The United States hockey
team was not supposed to have a chance in 1980. The Soviet
Union seemed invincible and unbeatable. Their team included
elite professionals who had played together for years. The
Americans, on the other hand, had teammates who had never
played together. None of them were professionals; they had
come from colleges and universities across America.

The American victory over the Soviets in the medal round
seemed improbable, if not impossible.

According to the movie based on these unlikely heroes,
the turning point for the Americans came in a practice led by

Coach Herb Brooks. The coach was demanding, perhaps driven to a fault. Brooks was not happy with the play of the team, so he had the players skating sprints to the point of exhaustion.

Some of the assistant coaches were worried that the players would either pass out or quit. They urged Brooks to stop.

Brooks pressed forward.

During the practices, Brooks would ask a player who he played for. The player would respond proudly with the name of his college. Brooks was asking the same question during this practice of total exhaustion.

One of the hockey players, recalling Brooks' persistent question, looked up from his prostrate position after his last sprint. Gasping for breath, he declared, "I play for the United States of America."

It was the defining moment.

They got it.

They did not play for the disparate colleges from which they came. They played for the United States of America.

And the team responded. They would beat the mighty Soviets in the first game of the medal round, and they would ultimately beat Finland for the gold medal.

Some say the victory over the Soviet Union was the greatest Olympic victory ever for the Americans. Others say it was the greatest moment in American sports. Most everyone who was alive in 1980 still remembers "the miracle on ice."

The Churches Did Not Get It

The American hockey players got it. They not only knew the game they were playing; they knew for whom they were playing: "I play for the United States of America."

They clearly understood their purpose. They clearly understood how to carry out their purpose.

That is certainly not the case with those churches that were dying. When I interviewed former members of the deceased churches, they referred to their last years in sad and similar ways:

- "We were going through the motions."
- "Everything we did seemed to be like we were in a rut or bad routine."
- "We became more attached to our ways of doing church than we did asking the Lord what He wanted us to do."
- "We were playing a game called church. We had no idea what we were really supposed to be doing."
- "We stopped asking what we should be doing for fear that it would require too much effort or change."

Do you get the picture? The church was not really a church. It had no purpose. None of the members talked about fulfilling the Great Commission. None of the members spoke about carrying out the Great Commandment in the church. None ever came close to speaking with a burning passion about making a difference in the community.

The churches were purposeless. They were engaged in an activity called, "This is the way we've always done it."

None of the members asked what they should be doing; they were too busy doing what they've always done.

When the Church Has a Biblical Purpose

The Apostle Paul was always concerned about the churches, particularly those churches where he had an active role in its beginnings. The Philippian church was one of those churches. Though Paul does not pull punches when he needs to be firm, for most of the letter you read of his great love for the church.

Early in the letter he tells the members of the church at Philippi one of the main reasons he has such an unfading love for them:

> I give thanks to my God for every remembrance of you, always praying with joy for all of you in my every prayer, because of your partnership in the gospel from the first day until now. (Phil. 1:3–5)

Did you get that? Did you read clearly why he was so thankful, why he had so much joy? The last portion of the sentence answers these questions: ". . . because of your partnership in the gospel from the first day until now."

The church understood her purpose. The members at Philippi knew what they were supposed to do. They were to live the gospel. They were to proclaim the gospel. They were to partner with Paul in the gospel. Their purpose was totally and completely gospel-centered.

Paul took great joy in the way they grasped their purpose. And don't miss that last phrase: ". . . from the first day until now." The Philippian church members did not stop understanding their purpose. From the day the church started until the day Paul wrote the letter, they knew what they were supposed to do. So they lived the gospel and they shared the gospel.

But the dying churches, at some point in their history, forgot their purpose. Rarely could anyone point to a singular event or historical moment where the purpose was forgotten. It was a deadly and slow process. Attitudes shifted from gospel-centered and other-centered to self-centered. An outward focus became an inward obsession. Routines and traditions and rituals replaced the original purpose of being a gospel-driven people.

As the church lost her purpose, she slowly but surely began to die. The process was typically lengthy, but death did come.

A church without a gospel-centered purpose is no longer a church at all.

Prayerful Commitment 10

God, reignite the hearts of our church members, including me, to have a passion for the gospel. Teach our church to share the gospel with others. Teach us to live as men and women who are true bearers of the good news of Jesus Christ. Remind us of our purpose. Convict us of our purpose. Empower us to live our purpose.

Questions for Prayerful Thought

1. Using the illustration of the United States Olympic hockey team of 1980, explain the need in dying churches to rediscover their purpose.

2. How can routine and tradition get in the way of a church fulfilling her purpose?

3. What did Paul mean in Philippians 1:3–5 when he thanked the church for her *partnership* in the gospel?

CHAPTER 11

The Church Obsessed
Over the Facilities

Of the fourteen deceased churches, I was able to see the former facilities of only one of them. Several had been razed; new and impressive buildings now sit where they once were. A couple of them were behind hastily erected fences. They had been condemned and any attempt to enter the property was illegal.

One of the churches, however, had neither been sold nor condemned. It sat on the property as it had for decades past. The former elder of the deceased church still had a key. He allowed me to go with him into the abandoned building. There was something he wanted me to see.

"There is really no market for the property," he said as we entered. "I'm not sure what will ultimately happen here. It will probably be like many of the buildings around town—abandoned and neglected."

I had expected cobwebs and piles of dust. To be sure, *Good Housekeeping* would not grant it the seal of approval. But it was tolerable. I got the impression that someone did light cleaning in the abandoned building on an occasional basis, much like one cleaning around a grave marker in a cemetery.

There were no utilities for the building, so he led me with a large flashlight. He walked confidently and quickly. He knew his way around.

We stopped. The light pointed to a room, a single room. "This is it," he said softly. I could not tell if his tone was respect or sadness.

The sign was still on the room: *Lydia Room.*

"This room was the equivalent of a parlor or bride's room in other churches," he offered without any questions from me. "There was a great pride about this room," he said. "It had the nicest furniture. It got first attention before anything else in the church."

He continued his story, and it was sadly typical. The room would become the focus of dissension. Who could use it? Who decided what furniture went in there? Could people outside the church use it? Could a normal church fellowship be held there?

"The arguments were pretty ugly," he said. "And I don't think I knew it at the time, but looking back, our focus on this room marked the beginning of our steep decline."

He paused. "I know we died for a lot of reasons," he offered, "but the fights over this room are the clearest markers I have that point to the closing of the doors. It seems so silly, so sad now. We were fighting over a stupid room while the church died."

The Obsession Reality

Sadly this elder's story is all too common. One church split and eventually died when the old pulpit was replaced with a new one. The church actually had a business meeting and a major battle to vote on the new pulpit. Members who had not been in church for years showed up for the vote. Indeed the so-called inactive members often became active for a contested business meeting in the dying churches. Their presence ended abruptly once the vote was over.

The "new pulpit" group defeated the "old pulpit" group in a close vote. The "old pulpit" group took the pulpit and started a new church. I resisted a series of one-liners about the possible name for the new church, because the story is pathetically sad and true.

By the way, the new church died only two years after its start. The older church held on for another eleven years before its demise.

A number of the fourteen churches became focused on memorials. Do not hear my statement as a criticism of memorials. I recently funded a memorial in memory of my grandson. I understand the emotional draw they have. Memorials come in the form of chairs, tables, rooms, and other places where a neat plaque can be placed.

The point is not the memorials themselves; the point is that memorials became an obsession at many of these churches. More and more emphasis was placed on the past, and the future was neglected.

The stories are, unfortunately, unending. In one church, a family funded the refurbishment and remodeling of a medium-sized meeting room. Years after that donation, extended family members changed the lock on the room and made unilateral decisions on who could use it.

Church fights have erupted over stained glass windows, pews, draperies, paint color, carpet color, and on and on and on. Dying churches, more often than not, experience severe battles over facility obsession before their demise.

Ironically, many of these churches were not obsessed about all of the facilities. Most of the building could be deteriorating noticeably, but they would still hang on and protect that one item or area.

Being a good steward of those material things that God has given our churches is good. Becoming obsessed with any one item to the neglect of His mission is idolatry.

Jesus and "Things"

Jesus was very clear on any obsession with material things. He preached the greatest message ever, the Sermon on the Mount. Right after He spoke about the eternal value of prayer and fasting, He chided the listeners who were obsessed with material and temporal items.

In Matthew 6:19–21, He said:

> Don't collect for yourselves treasures on earth, where moth and rust destroy and where thieves break in and steal. But collect for yourselves treasures in heaven, where neither moth nor rust destroys, and where thieves don't break in and steal. For where your treasure is, there your heart will be also.

Jesus' words apply to all of us. We are to be good stewards of personal finances and possessions. Likewise, we are to be good stewards of the material items in our churches. But if we focus on "things," no matter how meaningful they are, so that we become distracted from the eternal, we have lost our focus.

And a church that has lost her eternal focus is one step closer to dying and death.

Prayerful Commitment 11

Lord, teach me the proper stewardship of all the material items You give me personally and in my church. Help me never let that stewardship evolve into obsession and idolatry, especially where I lose my perspective on what really matters.

Questions for Prayerful Thought

1. Explain the difference between a church being a good steward over physical things versus the church becoming obsessed and idolatrous about them. What are some examples of each?

2. Why do so many churches have conflicts over "things"?

3. Look at Jesus' words in Matthew 6:19–21 and explain how they apply to a church either thriving or dying. What are examples of how churches can be obedient to His words: "But collect for yourselves treasures in heaven, where neither moth nor rust destroys, and where thieves don't break in and steal"?

PART 2

Is There Hope for the Dying Church?

Twelve Responses

CHAPTER 12

My Church Has Symptoms of Sickness: Four Responses

Though this book is brief, the path to get to this point must seem arduous. A lot of negative information has been communicated up to this point. I really don't know how I could have done otherwise. This book is an autopsy. I am trying to discern why churches died. It's hard to be bright and cheerful when you are talking about decay, dying, and death.

These final three chapters might not seem as dismal. I do offer some degree of hope and solutions for churches that are still alive.

But please hear me clearly.

These are no magical, easy-fix solutions. The twelve responses I offer over three chapters are not a recipe to create or repair the perfect church. To the contrary, they are more of a cry to God to intervene, and to create a willingness on the part of the church members to be obedient.

It's serious stuff. It's sobering.

The Path

As we go through these final chapters, I will address three types of churches: churches that have symptoms of sickness; very sick churches; and dying churches. And if we were to estimate the number of churches in each category, I would offer the following:

- Healthy: 10%
- Symptoms of sickness: 40%
- Very sick: 40%
- Dying: 10%

Though these numbers are not precise, I do believe they reflect the actual condition of churches across America. In this chapter, we will look at the first group of churches that make up roughly 40 percent of the American church population. These are churches in early but clear stages of sickness.

What Are the Symptoms of Sickness?

There are probably over 150,000 churches that fit this category. Though the process is imprecise, one of the signs that sickness might be taking hold includes a pervasive attitude in the church that the best days are in the past. If you were to ask longer-term members about the best days of the church, very few would recognize the present in that light.

While numbers are not everything, they can be telling from a symptomatic perspective. Churches with symptoms of sickness are likely to have declined some in worship attendance over the past five years. If they have grown, the rate of growth was slower than the growth rate of the community in which they are located. Many leaders stop looking at numbers when they began to decline. And when numbers are ignored, they tend to get even worse.

The ministries and programs for these churches tend to be shifting more and more for members of the congregation rather than those on the outside. In simple terms, the church is moving from an outward focus to an inward focus.

While some new members may be added each year, there is no sense of true disciple-making taking place. In fact, most of these churches do not have any clear plan for making disciples.

Finally, though by no means exhaustively, the church has a lot of program and ministry clutter. There is much busyness and activity, but a great deal of it has no meaningful purpose.

Most of these activities contribute little or nothing to the making of disciples. The primary reason those programs and ministries are continued is simply because "that's the way we've always done it."

Four Responses

In each of the final chapters, I will offer four of the twelve responses for each of the categories of the church. At the risk of redundancy, please hear that these are not quick-fix solutions. They are major categorical responses that must be adapted for each church.

1. *Pray that God will open the eyes of the leadership and members for opportunities to reach into the community where the church is located.* Jesus told His followers in Jerusalem just before His ascension that they were to be witnesses: "But you will receive power when the Holy Spirit has come upon you, and you will be My witnesses in Jerusalem, in all Judea and Samaria, and to the ends of the earth" (Acts 1:8). The first mandate is to impact your local community. Most churches with symptoms of sickness have become more inwardly focused.

2. *Take an honest audit of how church members spend their time being involved.* In most of these churches, the members are involved in ministries for themselves,

often to the exclusion of ministries beyond the church. The church loses outward momentum when the members start forming holy huddles.

3. *Take an audit of how the church spends its money.* Again, as churches become ill, they are more likely to use funds for their own members rather than reaching their community. Balance is the key, and most of these churches are out of balance.

4. *Make specific plans to minister and to evangelize your community.* You have prayed about it. You have honestly evaluated your time in programs and ministry, and how the church spends its funds. Now is the time to develop specific and concrete plans to impact the community. One church leader I know went to the principal of a nearby public elementary school. He asked the principal what the school needed most. That next summer, over 100 members of the church were painting walls in the school. The community ministries grew from that one commitment.

Prayerful Commitment 12

Lord, let me see my church with honesty and open eyes. Help me to grasp where we have gotten out of balance with inward and outward ministries. And give our church a vision to make a difference in our community. Even more, God, use me to be a catalyst and instrument for the changes that must take place in our church.

Questions for Prayerful Thought

1. In this chapter you read about churches that were beginning to show signs of sickness. What are some of those signs? What are other possible signs? Does your church have any signs of sickness?

2. Summarize the four responses for churches that are showing signs of sickness. What other responses could be added to these four?

3. What is the context of Acts 1:8? How can it be applicable and relevant to churches today with early signs of sickness?

CHAPTER 13

My Church Is Very Sick:
Four Responses

Frank was a member of the first church I served as pastor. I never knew him, but I heard his story several times.

The church was very small and very rural. Everyone in the church knew everyone who had ever attended the church.

Frank, I was told, began to develop symptoms of his sickness several years before his death. He was occasionally exhorted to go to the doctor, but he refused. Perhaps his rugged and independent ways could explain his behavior. I often wondered to myself if the poverty in the rural community kept people from seeking medical help.

Whatever the reasons, Frank got sicker and still refused help. His condition deteriorated for over two years before he sought medical attention. And he only sought help because the illness was so severe that he could not work. Frank had to get back to work on his small farm.

After about two days of tests, he and his wife got the grim results. He had developed an illness that, when caught in time, can easily be treated. Indeed, some patients had the disease for a year before they sought treatment, and they are fine today.

But Frank waited over two years. He waited until he was very sick. He would be declared terminal a year later.

Then he died.

So many times his grieving widow would tell me that he would be alive today if he had just seen a doctor earlier. I felt her grief. I felt her guilt.

Churches That Get Very Sick

Rarely does a church move from the category of "symptoms of sickness" to "very sick" overnight. It's more of a continuum. That is why it's so hard to detect and to respond if you're close to the church. From one day to the next, nothing seems to change. But there is an underlying deterioration taking place. Without intervention, the situation only gets worse.

There is no clearly defining moment when we can declare a church has moved into the "very sick" category. The church is more like Frank, where the conditions worsen gradually but progressively over time.

And if the church waits until it's very sick, it is extremely difficult to get better.

We estimate that, like the churches with symptoms of sickness, very sick churches comprise 40 percent of the number of American congregations. As a reminder, that is over 150,000 churches.

So what are some of the indicators that a church is very sick? Again, terminology and definitions are imprecise, but here are some of the more notable signs:

- Significant numerical decline over the past ten to twenty years. Most of the time we measure worship attendance for this metric.
- Prolonged times of apathy. Occasional times of intense conflict. The church seems more apathetic than anything else, but conflict can arise with surprising intensity.
- The church is not known in the community. Ask a clerk at a store in the community. You may be surprised how few even know the church exists.
- New members are rare. The exodus clearly exceeds the inflow.
- Revolving door of pastors. Frustration and conflict limit the years of pastoral tenure.
- The "good old days" are typically twenty or more years in the past. There has been a long season since anyone felt really good about the church.

Very sick churches do not have to manifest all of these symptoms, but they typically have at least three of them.

The challenge with the very sick churches is like the challenge presented with Frank. Once they move to this stage, reversal of the deterioration is incredibly difficult. Had the members recognized the problems earlier, help is more likely to be beneficial.

Sadly it's rare to see a church that is very sick reverse its course. Over time, the churches move to the terminal stage and eventually die. To be sure, that time frame can be very long. Churches as institutions fight tenaciously before closing the doors. But the reality of it is that many of the churches have ceased to be the church even though they appear open for service.

Four Responses

I love to be a dispenser of hope. But I refuse to be a dispenser of false hope. The current reality is that most of the churches in this category are headed for dying and death. Again, the process may be long, but it seems so inevitable for many.

Where is the hope in God? Do I not believe He can perform the miracles necessary to reverse the courses of these churches?

Of course I do. But in Scripture, God usually works with a willing people, at least a willing leader. When He delivered the Jews from the bondage of Egypt, He had a leader named Moses. That leader was initially reluctant, but eventually he obeyed and the people followed.

The rebuilding of Jerusalem was not easy after the exile, but God used Nehemiah to lead in the rebuilding of the wall around the city. He used Haggai to lead in the rebuilding of the temple.

Yes, reversal is possible, but God usually waits for a willing leader who will find willing people.

What are, then, some responses church leaders and members can have in their church if it is very sick? Again, I offer four broad categories.

1. *The church must admit and confess its dire need.* Most churches move toward death because they refuse to acknowledge their condition. Sometimes a single leader will be used of God to move the church in this positive direction.

2. *The church must pray for wisdom and strength to do whatever is necessary.* The change will not be easy.

3. *The church must be willing to change radically.* Frankly, this is usually the point of greatest resistance. The church has to change decades of cumulative problem behaviors in a very short time.

4. *That change must lead to action and an outward focus.* When a church begins to act positively with this radical change, it has essentially become a new church.

Can the reversal take place? It is highly unlikely. But it is not hopeless. Our hope is built upon the words of Jesus after He confronted the rich young man who wanted to enter the Kingdom of God:

"With men this is impossible, but with God all things are possible." (Matt. 19:26)

Prayer Commitment 13

I believe all things are possible through You, God. Show me what I need to do to lead my church from hopeless to hope. And give me the courage and strength to make those changes, even those changes that will be very painful.

Questions for Prayerful Thought

1. What are the symptoms of a very sick church? Does your church have any of these symptoms?

2. Read Haggai 1. How does the story of the rebuilding of the temple relate to reversing the course of a very sick church?

3. Where does a very sick church begin if its members and leaders truly desire reversal? What sacrifices must be made? What comforts must be given up?

CHAPTER 14

My Church Is Dying: Four Responses

D^{eath.}
  Dying.

Those are subjects most of us like to avoid. But, unless Jesus returns before our death, it is the inevitable path for all of us. Instead of acting like it doesn't exist, we should embrace our earthly mortality in a way that brings the most glory to God.

Many of you have walked with someone who is dying. My first experience was with my father. I was twenty-eight years old. I did not want to accept what I had been told.

After denial, I began to have resentment about my perceived unfairness of it all. I had two little boys, ages two and four. The third son would not be born for another year. I wanted my dad to see his grandchildren grow up. I wanted the incredible influence he had been on my life to be available for my sons.

I guess I was selfish. I wanted my dad to live for me. I needed him. I needed his calm assurances. I needed his advice. I needed his love. I just wanted my dad to live.

I was twenty-eight years old. I thought my dad would be with me for a few more decades. He was too young to die. It just was not fair. He had survived awful wounds in World War II. He won the Purple Heart and other medals. Why would God allow this cancer to take him when He had protected him so well in the past?

I refused to accept that my dad was dying.

He was my hero.

He was my best friend.

The Conversation

It would be the last meaningful conversation I would have with my dad. Instead of my ministering to him, he ministered to me. That was unfair too. That was selfish of me.

He knew I needed to hear these words from him. He told me how and when he became a follower of Christ. He told me how he went to war, never asking God to spare him. He told me how he made a commitment to God to give his future children to the service of the Lord if he did return and marry my mother.

He looked at me with total love and piercing eyes of truth. "Thom," he began. "You and your brother are the answers to my prayers. My life is complete. I can go now. I will be fine."

I did not let him go immediately. It would be a process over the next few weeks. But the releasing of my father began that day.

Death came into the world with the sin of man. Eternal life came into the world with death and resurrection of Jesus.

Dad died. It was the first funeral I ever officiated.

I let him go.

The Death of a Church

No one wants his or her church to die. No one desires to let go of the church he loves. No one wants to lose the church to which she gave so many years.

But churches die. Certainly the universal church will never die. Jesus made that abundantly clear. He said, "On this rock I will build My church, and the forces of Hades will not overpower it" (Matt. 16:18).

But individual congregations die.

Your church may be one of those dying churches. I have taken the length of this short book to describe the symptoms of those churches.

And you may have been like I was with my father. It's not happening. Denial.

But now it's time to let go. Holding on will do no one any good. A dying church is of little benefit to the Kingdom . . . unless it dies well.

How might a church die well? Allow me to offer four responses as I conclude this little tome. And allow me to suggest four ways you can be a part of a church that dies with dignity.

Four Responses: Death with Dignity

If you have truly acknowledged that your church is dying, what can you and the few members who remain do? What can you do in the last days of your congregation to make sure that your church's death can actually make a difference for good for the Kingdom? Here are four options.

1. *Sell the property and give the funds to another church, perhaps a new church that has begun or will soon begin.* You can be assured that the death of your church helped another church to live.

2. *Give the building to another church.* New churches are starting by the thousands every month in America. One of their greatest challenges is to find a place where they can meet.

3. *If your church is in a transitional neighborhood, turn over the leadership and property to those who actually reside in the neighborhood.* A few Anglo churches are beginning

to do so where the neighborhood is now predominantly African American or another ethnic group.

4. *Merge with another church, but let the other church have the ownership and leadership of your church.* In simple terms, you are allowing the healthy church to take over your church. That is sacrificial. That is a way to die with dignity.

All of these options are painful, because all of the options are truly sacrificial. What you are doing is allowing your church to die so that another may live.

In doing so, you are following the example of the One who made the ultimate sacrifice with His death.

And that is the very best example to follow.

Prayerful Commitment 14

Lord, if it is Your will for our church to die, please let me know. And give me the courage and the strength to let go. For Your glory.

Questions for Prayerful Thought

1. How does Matthew 16:18 relate to dying churches?

2. What are four ways a dying church can offer life to another church?

3. Above all, what have you learned from this brief book? What has God taught you as you read these chapters?

A Note from Thom:

I invite you to join me each day for a new article at my blog, ThomRainer.com. I welcome interaction and comments on the blog, and I respond to many of them throughout the day.